WEEKLY WR READER®
EARLY LEARNING LIBRARY

Great Americans
Crispus Attucks

Monica L. Rausch

Reading consultant: Susan Nations, M.Ed., author/literacy coach/
consultant in literacy development

Please visit our web site at: **www.garethstevens.com**
For a free color catalog describing Weekly Reader® Early Learning Library's list
of high-quality books, call 1-877-445-5824 (USA) or 1-800-387-3178 (Canada).
Weekly Reader® Early Learning Library's fax: (414) 336-0164.

Library of Congress Cataloging-in-Publication Data

Rausch, Monica.
    Crispus Attucks / by Monica L. Rausch.
        p. cm. — (Great Americans)
    Includes bibliographical references and index.
    ISBN-13: 978-0-8368-7681-9 (lib. bdg.)
    ISBN-13: 978-0-8368-7688-8 (softcover)
        1. Attucks, Crispus, d. 1770—Juvenile literature. 2. African Americans—
Biography—Juvenile literature. 3. Revolutionaries—Massachusetts—
Boston—Biography—Juvenile literature. 4. Boston Massacre, 1770—
Juvenile literature. I. Title.
    E185.97.A86R38   2007
    973.3'113092—dc22
    [B]   2006032577

This edition first published in 2007 by
Weekly Reader® Early Learning Library
A Member of the WRC Media Family of Companies
330 West Olive Street, Suite 100
Milwaukee, WI 53212 USA

Copyright © 2007 by Weekly Reader® Early Learning Library

Managing editor: Valerie J. Weber
Art direction: Tammy West
Cover design and page layout: Charlie Dahl
Picture research: Sabrina Crewe
Production: Jessica Yanke and Robert Kraus

Picture credits: Cover, title page © Hulton Archive/Getty Images; pp. 5, 6, 9, 17 © The Granger Collection,
New York; pp. 7, 15 © CORBIS; pp. 10, 11, 14, 18, 20 © North Wind Picture Archives; p. 13 National Park
Service/Boston National Historical Park; p. 16 Library of Congress; p. 21 © 2006 Stanley Rowin

Printed in the United States of America

1 2 3 4 5 6 7 8 9 10 10 09 08 07 06

Table of Contents

Cover and title page: Crispus Attucks was a brave man. He was not afraid of British soldiers.

Chapter 1

From Slavery to Freedom

Crispus Attucks was the first American to die in the United States' fight for independence. Attucks died in a fight called the Boston **Massacre**, along with four other people. The death of Attucks and the other men made people angry. After they died, many people all over America wanted to fight for independence.

Crispus Attucks was born in 1723 in Framingham, near Boston, Massachusetts. His mother was a Native American. His father was from Africa. Because his father was a **slave**, Attucks was also a slave.

When Attucks was old enough, he helped his owner buy and sell cattle. Attucks had some freedom, but he wanted to work for himself. He did not want to remain a slave. Attucks wanted to work on ships.

British soldiers shot at Crispus Attucks (*lower right*) and other Americans during the Boston Massacre.

Attucks left Boston on a whaling ship like this one. These sailors are cutting apart the whale to use its oil and other parts.

In 1750, when Attucks was twenty-seven, he ran away. He went to work on a **whaling ship**. The ship sailed out to sea. Attucks's owner, William Brown, could not find Attucks. Brown offered people money to find him and bring him back, but no one could find Attucks. Finally, Brown stopped looking for him.

Attucks was finally free! For the next twenty years, he worked on ships as a sailor. When Attucks was not at sea, he worked as a rope maker.

Some ships at the Boston **docks** were whaling ships. Other ships carried food, cloth, and other things to sell.

Chapter 2

British Soldiers on Boston Streets

Massachusetts was a colony. Massachusetts and the other American colonies had to obey the laws of Great Britain. In 1767, Great Britain passed a law that made Americans angry. The law taxed some goods.

In 1768, the governor of Massachusetts was worried. He thought people were getting too angry about the tax. He asked the British king to send soldiers. The governor wanted the soldiers to protect the people who collected taxes.

King George III wanted to keep the American colonies for Britain. He sent British soldiers to America.

© North Wind Picture Archives

Attucks and other sailors and rope makers did not like the soldiers. When the soldiers were off duty, they worked at other jobs. One of the jobs was rope making. People started hiring the British soldiers to make rope. Attucks and the other American rope makers had a hard time finding jobs.

British soldiers marched through Boston's streets in 1768. There were so many soldiers in Boston that they did not have enough places to stay. Some slept in tents in the middle of the city.

Other people in Boston did not like the soldiers, either. Seeing the soldiers reminded the people that the British king was in charge. The soldiers bossed people around. People became more and more angry. Something was going to happen soon!

Sometimes the soldiers had to live in people's homes. The people did not like the soldiers staying with them. They used their beds and ate their food!

Chapter 3

The Boston Massacre

On March 5, 1770, something really did happen! Some boys started teasing a British soldier in Boston. They called him names. The soldier hit one of the boys with the end of his gun. People around the boy grew angry. Many people started gathering on the city streets.

Attucks was on the docks working with other sailors. He heard about the people gathering in the streets. He started to lead a group of sailors to the town square in front of the Old State House.

The Old State House was a government building in the center of Boston. Today, the brick circle marking the site of the Boston Massacre lies in front of it.

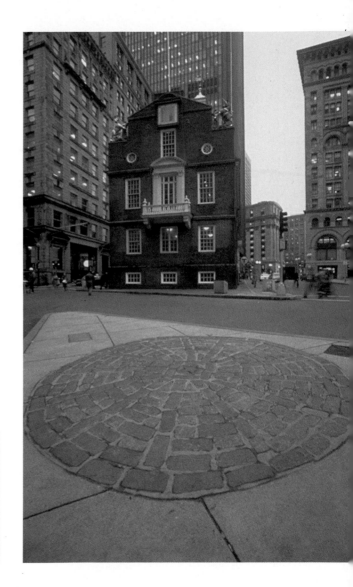

13

© North Wind Picture Archives

The British soldier called his officer, and the officer gathered eight soldiers in the town square. The soldiers were afraid the people might hurt them.

The British soldiers knew many people did not like them. People sometimes yelled at them on the streets.

Somebody rang a church bell. Usually the bell only rang when there was a fire. Many people thought a fire had started, and they came to help put it out. When they got to the town square, however, they did not see flames. They joined the crowd of people yelling at the soldiers.

The Christ Church, or Old North Church, in Boston had the first church bells in North America. The bells were rung for church services or when there was a fire.

When Attucks arrived, some people were throwing snowballs and rocks at the soldiers. Some people were daring the soldiers to shoot. No one knows exactly what happened next. Some people said Attucks was holding a stick. Others said he was holding a club. Some said he struck a soldier's gun. Others said he did not hit the gun.

The soldiers were nervous. They were ready to start shooting!

Some people said they heard a voice yell "Fire!" One of the soldiers fired, and he shot Attucks. The other soldiers began to shoot. When they stopped firing, Attucks and two other men were dead. Two more men died later from their wounds. Six other people were also hurt. After the shooting, the British officer and the soldiers left Boston.

Crispus Attucks was the first person the soldiers killed. Samuel Gray, a rope maker, and James Caldwell, a sailor also died that day. Samuel Maverick and Patrick Carr died later. Maverick was only seventeen years old.

© North Wind Picture Archives

Some people thought Attucks and his men were heroes. Others thought they were just part of a mob. A man named Samuel Adams wanted people to get excited and to get angry at the British soldiers. He called the shootings the "Boston Massacre."

Thousands of people came to the men's funeral. They made a big procession to the cemetery. Stores were closed, and bells rang.

Samuel Adams said the British troops should leave Boston.

18

Chapter 4

Honoring the Victims

The soldiers who shot Attucks and the other men were arrested. They were accused of murder. The soldiers said that the crowd was dangerous. They said that they had shot at Attucks and the other men because they were afraid. They believed people in the crowd were going to attack them.

After their trial, six of the soldiers were set free. Only two soldiers were punished.

For the next six years, people honored March 5 as the day of the Boston Massacre. On July 18, 1776, the **Declaration of Independence** was read in Boston. It was read from the Old State House balcony, above the place where Attucks was shot.

Many people came to hear the Declaration of Independence. They were ready to fight the British!

© North Wind Picture Archives

In 1888, a statue was built in the Boston Common, a park. The statue honors Attucks. In 1998, the United States government made a special coin to honor Attucks and other African Americans who fought for American independence.

The names of the victims of the Boston Massacre are carved at the top of this statue in the Boston Common. Their grave is in the Granary Burying Ground next to the park.

Glossary

accused — blamed for doing a crime

colony — the land and people ruled by another country

Declaration of Independence — the statement made by the American colonies telling Great Britain that the colonies were free

docks — places along a shore where ships can come to load and unload goods

massacre — the act of killing many people who do not or cannot fight back

mob — a crowd of people acting out of control, often damaging property or hurting other people

off duty — not at work as a soldier or sailor

procession — a group of people walking an an organized way

slave — a person treated as property and forced to work without pay

taxed — charged a fee or sum of money by the government. The government uses the money to pay its workers and to pay for other government costs.

whaling ship — a ship that is used to hunt whales

For More Information

Books

The Cost of Freedom: Crispus Attucks and the Boston Massacre. Great Moments in American History (series). Joanne Mattern (Rosen Publishing)

Crispus Attucks: Hero of the Boston Massacre. Famous People in American History (series). Anne Beier (Rosen)

Crispus Attucks. Heroes of the American Revolution (series). Don McLeese (Rourke)

Explore Black History with Wee Pals. Morrie Turner (Just Us Books)

Web Sites

Boston Massacre Historical Society
www.bostonmassacre.net/pictures/index.htm
Click on pictures to see drawings of the Boston Massacre

Father Ryan High School: Crispus Attucks
www.fatherryan.org/blackmilitary/attucks.htm
Short biography of Crispus Attucks

Publisher's note to educators and parents: Our editors have carefully reviewed these Web sites to ensure that they are suitable for children. Many Web sites change frequently, however, and we cannot guarantee that a site's future contents will continue to meet our high standards of quality and educational value. Be advised that children should be closely supervised whenever they access the Internet.

Index

About the Author

Monica L. Rausch has a master's degree in creative writing from the University of Wisconsin-Milwaukee, where she is currently teaching composition, literature, and creative writing. She likes to write fiction, but sticking to the facts is fun, too. Monica lives in Milwaukee near her six nieces and nephews, to whom she loves to read books.